KiDS COOKING

TASTY RECIPES
with Step-by-Step PHOTOS

by the editors of KLUTZ

KLUTZ®

CONTENTS

FAMILY DINNER

DESSERTS

the KITCHEN RULES!

We here at Klutz believe that the kitchen is a very special room in your house, with special rules. The most important of which is **RULE #1.**

Make sure to have oven mitts and a heat-proof surface to handle any hot pots and pans!

1 BE CAREFUL!

The **GROWN-UP ASSISTANT** and the **kid chef** should talk about any recipe before you start it. If the recipe calls for a **knife**, a **hot stove**, or an **oven**, the **GROWN-UP ASSISTANT** should always do those tasks. Use the grown-up's judgment when the kid chef is ready to take on more responsibility in the kitchen. Oh, and it's not a bad idea to have a **fire extinguisher** on hand. Just in case.

GROWN-UPS!
Look for this symbol when it's your turn to do something in the recipe. Always supervise kid chefs in the kitchen. Never leave a child unattended.

GROWN-UP ASSISTANT

Kid Chef

2 **BE CLEAN!** Cooking is a lot of fun, but you won't get to do it very often if you leave a mess behind. If your recipe makes you **wait**, why not wash some dirty dishes as you go? When you finish cooking, **clean up everything** and **put it away.** You'll keep your **GROWN-UP ASSISTANT** a lot happier.

Wash the rainbow whisk really well before using it. The whisk is dishwasher safe.

3 **BE READY!**
Look over the **ingredient list** and see if you have everything. If you don't, talk to your **ASSISTANT** to see if you can substitute with something else. Also make sure that **none** of the ingredients will cause an **allergic reaction** to you or anyone you're cooking for.

B R E A K F A S T

Buried Treasure
Muffins

Create a tasty surprise for your breakfast buddies to discover!

YOU WILL NEED

1 cup (140g)
all-purpose flour

1/2 cup (45 g)
quick oats

1/4 cup (50 mL)
sugar

2 tsp (10 mL)
baking powder

1/2 tsp (2.5 mL)
salt

1 egg

3/4 cup (180 mL)
milk

1/4 cup (60 mL)
vegetable oil

3/4 cup (180 mL) jam or
other fillings (see page 11)

2 mixing bowls

Rainbow whisk

8 paper
muffin cups

Muffin tin

Turn the page for the recipe.

— HOW TO —
MEASURE

Use the back of a knife to "level off" the top of your ingredients.

Not like this . . .

Just like this . . .

9

GROWN-UPS!
Do Step 1.

1. PREHEAT YOUR OVEN TO 400°F (205°C). In a big **mixing bowl**, stir together all the DRY ingredients: **flour**, **quick oats**, **sugar**, **baking powder**, and **salt**. Then dig a little hole in the middle of it all.

2. In **another bowl**, mix the WET ingredients. Break the **egg** and mix it with the **milk** and **oil**.

3. Pour the **wet mixture** into the **dry mixture** to make the batter. Stir the batter until everything is mixed, but don't stir it too long. Leave it a little lumpy.

TIP
If you don't use paper liners, make sure to grease the tin really well.

4. Place a **paper muffin cup** in each hole of the **tin**. Fill the muffin cups halfway with batter. Then put a teaspoon (tsp) of **jam** in the center, leaving batter all around. Then add just enough batter to cover the jam.

GROWN-UPS!
Do Step 5.

5. Bake in a 400°F oven for **20–25 minutes**. Get your **GROWN-UP ASSISTANT'S** help to take them out with oven mitts and set the tin on a heatproof surface.

MIX UP YOUR MIX-INS!

You can also use . . .

NUT BUTTER

COOKIE BUTTER

CHOCOLATE CHIPS

. . . instead of jam.

Make sure none of your guests are allergic to any of the treasures, of course.

Or instead of filling the **muffins** with **jam**, chop up fruit, like **apples**, **peaches**, or **strawberries**. Gently mix the fruit pieces into the batter after you mix in the wet ingredients.

SCRAMBLED  EGG
BUDDIES

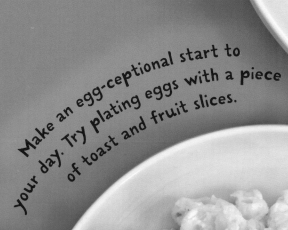
Make an egg-ceptional start to your day. Try plating eggs with a piece of toast and fruit slices.

2 eggs

2 tsp (10 mL) butter

Salt and pepper to taste

MAKES 1 BREAKFAST

Prep & Cook Time: 10 minutes

1 slice bread (optional)

Fruit slices (optional)

Small bowl

Rainbow whisk

Frying pan

Spatula

1. Crack the **eggs** into a **small bowl** and **whisk** them. Remove any bits of eggshell that fell in. Whisk the eggs until they look all the same color.

GROWN-UPS! Do Step 2.

✳2. Melt the **butter** in a **frying pan** over low heat (butter is easy to burn) and pour in the eggs. Push your **spatula** under the eggs and gently mix them so they cook evenly and don't stick to the bottom of the pan.

4. Shake on a little **salt** and **pepper**. Careful, not too much!

3. Different people like their eggs differently, so take yours out whenever they look done to you.

DID YOU KNOW...?
Short-order cooks have their own terms for different foods. "Wreck 'em!" means scrambled eggs.

COWBOY EGG

Wait, what?

There are many different names for this dish. Some people call it Egg in a Basket, Rocky Mountain Toast, or Toad in a Hole.

DID YOU KNOW...?
Scientists believe that chickens are the closest living relatives of the Tyrannosaurus rex!

4 tsp (20 mL) butter

1 slice of bread

Cookie cutter or drinking glass

1 egg

Spatula

Small bowl

Frying pan

MAKES 1 SERVING

Prep & Cook Time: 10 minutes

1. Cut a hole in the center of the **bread** with a **cookie cutter** or a small upside-down drinking glass.

GROWN-UPS! Do Steps 2 & 4.

✳2. Melt half the **butter** in a small **frying pan** over medium-low heat. Place the bread in the pan, and let it toast until the bottom is slightly golden. (Use a **spatula** to peek at the bottom.)

3. Flip the bread over with the spatula. Crack the **egg** into a bowl, and remove any bits of eggshell that fell in. Then pour the egg into the middle of the cutout bread.

✳4. Keep cooking until the egg looks good to you. If you want, you can flip the bread over with a spatula to fry the egg on both sides.

TIP: If you have room in the pan, cook the circle of bread that you cut out. Serve that little buttery nugget of bread on the side.

Snow Day Hot CHOCOLATE

TIP
Hide a nugget of chocolate in the bottom of each mug before you pour in the cocoa.

Did you spend all day sledding or building a snow fort because school was canceled? Then you need to make a cup of cocoa!

— YOU WILL NEED —

3 Tbsp (45 mL) cocoa powder

3 Tbsp (45 mL) sugar

1/2 tsp (2.5 mL) cinnamon (optional)

1/4 cup (60 mL) water

4 cups (1 L) of milk

About 25 mini marshmallows (optional)

Saucepan

Rainbow whisk

MAKES 4 SERVINGS
Prep & Cook Time: 15 minutes

1. Place the **cocoa powder, sugar, cinnamon** (if you like cinnamon), and **water** in the **saucepan**. Blend them with the **whisk** until the cocoa is all mixed in.

2. Slowly add the **milk** and stir them all together.

GROWN-UPS! Do Step 3.

✳ **3.** Set the saucepan over low heat. Keep stirring everything until it's hot.

4. Just before serving, beat the cocoa with the whisk to make it foamy. Add a few **mini marshmallows**.

— MAKE IT A — GIFT!

Multiply all the dry ingredients (cocoa, sugar, and cinnamon) by four, and put them in a jar. Stick a label on the jar with the instructions: Heat 1 1/2 Tbsp (22 mL) of cocoa mix and 1 Tbsp (15 mL) of water with 1 cup (250 mL) of milk.

Hot CHOCOLATE

1 1/2 Tablespoons Hot Chocolate Mix + 1 Tablespoon water + 1 cup warm milk

Find a premade label in the front of this book.

FRENCH TOAST
with Strawberry Butter

This breakfast takes a little more time, but it's perfect for a lazy weekend morning.

YOU WILL NEED:

MAKES 2–3 SERVINGS

Prep & Cook Time: 30 minutes

1/4 cup (60 mL) softened butter + extra to grease the pan

2 Tbsp (30 mL) confectioner's sugar

1/3 cup (80 mL) frozen or fresh strawberries with stems and leaves removed

2 eggs

1/2 cup (125 mL) milk

1 tsp (5 mL) cinnamon

4–6 slices of bread (slightly stale bread is best)

Blender

Shallow bowl

Rainbow whisk

Flat spatula

Frying pan

PEACH BUTTER
No strawberries? Use 1 large soft peach, pit and skin removed, instead.

strawberry butter

TIP
Leave your butter out of the fridge until it warms up to room temperature. It needs to be really soft to blend with the strawberries.

GROWN-UPS! Supervise the blender.

✳ **1.** Add 1/4 cup (60 mL) of **butter**, the **powdered sugar**, and the **strawberries** into a **blender.** Put the cover on the blender.

✳ **2.** Then whirl away till it's fluffy. If you're making the butter ahead of time, store the strawberry butter in an airtight container in the fridge.

french toast

Tip
Always wash your hands after handling raw eggs.

1. Break the **eggs** into a **shallow bowl**. Add the **milk** and **cinnamon**, then **whisk** them to make batter.

GROWN-UPS!
Do Steps 2 & 4.

2. Set the **frying pan** over medium heat. Drop a small piece of **butter** (about 2 tsp) into the pan, and move it around with a **spatula** to grease the whole bottom.

3. Dip the **bread slices**, one at a time, into the egg batter and turn them over. Don't try to soak them, just get them good and wet.

✳**4.** As the bread slices come out of the batter, put them onto the frying pan and cook both sides until golden brown. Use a spatula to peek underneath and make sure you don't burn the bottoms. You may need to re-grease the pan with more butter now and then.

5. Plate your French toast, and serve with **strawberry butter**. If it's a special occasion, add a little whipped cream or syrup.

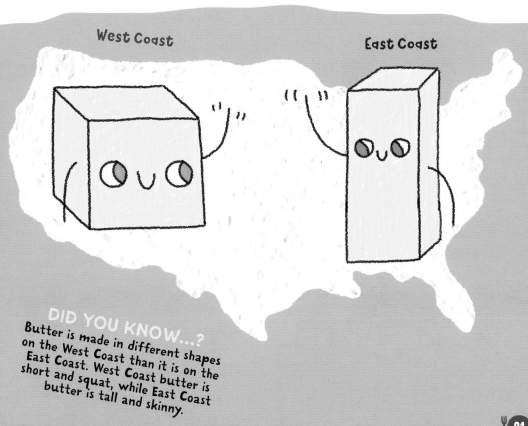

West Coast

East Coast

DID YOU KNOW....?
Butter is made in different shapes on the West Coast than it is on the East Coast. West Coast butter is short and squat, while East Coast butter is tall and skinny.

smoothies
~TWO WAYS~

Prep Time:
10 minutes

A fruity, frosty smoothie will give you a burst of energy on the blah-est of Monday mornings.

MAKES
1 JUMBO SMOOTHIE
—OR—
2 MEDIUM-SIZE SMOOTHIES

STEP 1

Pour the **liquid ingredients** (**orange juice** or **yogurt**) into the **blender**.

STEP 2

Put all the **fruit** in at once. Put the cover on the blender.

GROWN-UPS! Do Step 3.

*STEP 3

Turn the blender on and blend it until smooth.

STEP 4

Don't forget your silly straw!

Pour the smoothie into a **tall glass**. Enjoy!

STRAWBERRY BANANA smoothie

YOU WILL NEED

1 cup (250 mL) orange juice

1/2 cup (125 mL) vanilla yogurt

1 1/2 cups (375 mL) frozen strawberries

1 banana   Blender

RAZZLE-DAZZLE smoothie

YOU WILL NEED

1 1/2 cups (375 mL) orange juice

1 cup (250 mL) frozen raspberries

1 cup (250 mL) frozen mango chunks

Blender

LUNCH & SNACKS

Bugged-Out snack platter

MAKES
1 SHAREABLE
SNACK PLATTER

Prep Time:
20 minutes

Yikes! What's crawling all over the crudités?*

*Crudités (kroo-dee-**TAY**): raw veggies
cut into pieces for easy snacking

GROWN-UPS!
Do Steps 1 & 2.

STEP 1

Chop all your **veggies**. Cut the
celery stalk into pieces about
3 inches (7.5 cm) long. Slice the
cucumber into rounds, like crackers.

STEP 2

For ladybugs, cut **tomatoes** in half,
then cut a little notch into the back.
Cut the **olives** into slices.

STEP 3

Spread each piece with your **topping
of choice** (**peanut butter** or **cream
cheese**), using a **butter knife**.

STEP 4

Top them off with your bugs!
Put a few **raisins** on the peanut
butter for ants. Layer an olive
slice, then a tomato to make
one ladybug.

Did you know...?
About two in seven people around the
world eat actual insects and arachnids.
Some popular bugs include crickets,
ants, and even scorpions!

ANTS ON A LOG

YOU WILL NEED

1 celery stalk

2 Tbsp (30 mL) peanut butter

1 Tbsp (15 mL) raisins

Cutting board

Knife

Butter knife

TIP: If you don't eat peanut butter, you can spread cream cheese on the celery.

LADYBUG ON A LEAF

YOU WILL NEED

1 English cucumber

1/4 cup (60 ml) cherry tomatoes

2 Tbsp (30 mL) black olives

2 Tbsp (30 mL) cream cheese

Cutting board

Knife

Butter knife

SNACK STACKERS

SWITCH UP YOUR FLAVOR COMBOS!

SAVORY ANTS ON A LOG:
Carrot stick + hummus + pine nuts

SWEET LADYBUGS:
Green apple slice + jam + strawberry and grape slices

FRUIT RAINBOW KEBABS

Stack up a skewer with your own crazy, colorful creation!

YOU WILL NEED

1/4 cup (60 mL) purple grapes

2 Tbsp (30 mL) blueberries

1 kiwi

1/4 cup (60 mL) fresh pineapple pieces

1/4 cup (60 mL) mango pieces

1/2 cup (125 mL) strawberries

6 bamboo skewers

Sticker flags (optional)

GROWN-UPS! Do Step 1.

STEP 1

Wash and dry the **grapes**, **blueberries**, and **strawberries**. De-stem the strawberries. A grown-up can peel and slice the **kiwi** into six pieces.

GROWN-UPS! Do Step 2.

STEP 2

With the pointy end facing away from you, add the fruit one at a time to the **skewers** in rainbow order. Start with the purple grapes, and end with the strawberries (or vice-versa).

STEP 3

Peel off the **sticker flags** from the front of the book, and fold one over the non-pointy end of each skewer.

OVER THE (FRUIT) RAINBOW

Each fruit represents one color of the rainbow (red, orange, yellow, green, blue, purple). You can use any fruits you like if you don't have the fruits shown here. How many different fruits can you name that go with each color of the rainbow? (Blue is the trickiest!)

HOLY GUACAMOLE!

Nothing gets a party started better than a big batch of fresh guac.

— YOU WILL NEED —

1 green onion 1 tomato 3 ripe avocados ½ tsp (2.5 mL) garlic powder 1 Tbsp (15 mL) lemon juice (half of a fresh lemon)

Salt 1 bag tortilla chips Cutting board Knife Fork and Spoon Mixing bowl

GROWN-UPS! Do Steps 1 & 2.

1. Chop the **green onion** and **tomato** into small pieces.

2. Slice the **avocados** in half, and use a spoon to remove the big seeds (pits). Save one of the seeds for a science experiment.

3. Scoop the avocado insides into a bowl. Add the **garlic powder** and **lemon juice**. Mash it all up with a **fork**.

4. Add the chopped onion and tomato and a few shakes of **salt**. Mix everything together. Bring on the **tortilla chips**, and dig in!

— SCIENCE EXPERIMENT —
AVOCADO SPROUTING!

Carefully stick four toothpicks into the avocado seed. Balance it over a jar of water, with the pointed end up and the rounded end in the water. In about a week, you should see a little plant sprouting from the top. If your pit doesn't sprout in 6-8 weeks, try this experiment with another avocado.

HOORAH for HUMMUS!

This snack is perfect for vegging out!

Bonus: We included our top-secret trick for making garlic not-too-garlicky.

BROWN BAG LUNCH IDEAS

MONDAY = sushi burrito (page 38) + orange

TUESDAY = peanut butter & jelly sandwich + fruit kebabs (page 28)

WEDNESDAY = ants on a log (page 27) + string cheese

THURSDAY = turkey sandwich with guacamole (page 30) + apple

FRIDAY = bagel with hummus (page 32) + cherry tomatoes

— YOU WILL NEED —

MAKES 5–6 SERVINGS

Prep Time: 40 minutes

3 cloves garlic

15 oz (420 g) can of garbanzo beans

2 Tbsp (30 mL) plain Greek yogurt

2 Tbsp (30 mL) olive oil

2 Tbsp (30 mL) water

1 1/2 tsp (7.5 mL) lemon juice

1/2 tsp (2.5 mL) kosher salt

1/4 tsp (1.25 mL) cumin

Sliced Veggies

Saucepan

Spatula

Food processor

Tip

Save 2 Tbsp of water from the saucepan for extra garlic flavor in Step 4.

GROWN-UPS! DO STEPS 1, 3 & 4.

1. Add a few inches of **water** to your **saucepan**, bring it to a boil, and add the cloves of **garlic** (still in the skin). Cook them for 10–12 minutes, or until the cloves are tender.

2. While the garlic cooks, pop the skins off the **garbanzo beans**, one at a time. This is optional if you're short on time, but peeling makes your hummus smooth and creamy.

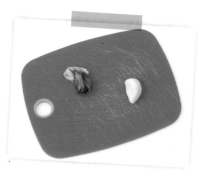

3. Take the saucepan off the heat and run cold water into the saucepan to cool the garlic. Once the garlic is totally cool, peel off the skins.

5. Scoop the hummus into a bowl for serving. Drizzle a little extra **olive oil** on top (if you like) and add an extra dash of cumin. Serve it with **sliced veggies**.

4. Add the peeled garlic and **chickpeas**, plus the **yogurt, olive oil, water, lemon juice, salt,** and **cumin** to the bowl of a **food processor**. Process the hummus for about 30 seconds, stopping to scrape down the hummus stuck to the sides with a **spatula**.

Real-Deal Lemonade

Some people say, "When life gives you lemons, make lemonade." We say, bring on the lemons!

MAKES 1 SERVING

Prep Time: 10 minutes

1 lemon

1 cup (250 mL) cold water

2 tsp (10 mL) sugar

Ice cubes   Cutting board   Knife   Bowl   Rainbow whisk

GROWN-UPS! Do Step 1.

1. Roll the **lemon** back and forth on a cutting board to make it easier to juice. Get your grown-up assistant to cut the lemon in half.

2. Squeeze the lemon pieces with your hands (or a juicer if you have one) over a **bowl**. Take out all the seeds, if any fell in.

3. Add the cup of **water** and **sugar**, and **whisk** it together.

4. Fill a glass with **ice cubes**, and pour the lemonade over the ice.

PiNK Lemonade

After you've squeezed your lemon juice, pour it into a blender and whirl it around with three or four strawberries (washed and without their green tops).

If you plan to sell your lemonade, gather these supplies.

LEMONADE STAND CHECKLIST

- ☐ Pitcher
- ☐ Cups
- ☐ Napkins
- ☐ Sign with price*
- ☐ Cash box with extra change

*A grown-up can help you set your price so it's higher than the cost of ingredients, cups, napkins, and anything else you bought for your business.

CHEESY
CATS-ADILLA

This might be the easiest hot lunch you'll ever make.

Flour or corn
tortilla

Handful of shredded
cheddar cheese

Salsa
(optional)

Sour cream
(optional)

Veggie slices
(optional)

Spatula

Nonstick or cast-iron
frying pan

GROWN-UPS!
Do Steps 1 & 2.

✳ **1.** Heat the **frying pan** over low heat, and warm a **tortilla** on one side for about 30 seconds. Then turn it over with a **spatula** and sprinkle with as much **shredded cheese** as you like.

✳ **2.** When the cheese has melted, use the spatula to put the tortilla on your plate and top with a scoop of **salsa** and a plop of **sour cream**, if you'd like.

3. Fold the tortilla in half. If you have some extra time, decorate the outside of the tortilla with **veggie slices**. (Get creative with the leftovers in your fridge!) We used pieces of carrot, black olives, cucumbers, tomatoes, and extra cheese shreds.

Did You Know...?

It takes about 10 lbs (4.5 kg) of milk to make 1 lb (½ kg) of cheese.

This burrito is inspired by the flavors of Hawaii and Japan.

Aloha Sushi Burrito

TIP
Sushi burritos can fall apart a little bit. That's OK! Wrap this burrito in wax paper before you pack it in your lunch box, then peel back the paper at lunchtime.

— YOU WILL NEED —

MAKES 1 BURRITO

Cook Time (Rice): 40 minutes

Prep Time (Burrito): 15 minutes

- 1½ cups (375 mL) medium-grain sushi rice
- 2 cups (500 mL) water
- 1 Tbsp (15 mL) seasoned-rice vinegar
- 1 slice of Black Forest ham
- 1 slice of fresh mozzarella
- 1 leaf of romaine heart
- 1½ oz (42 g) fresh pineapple
- 1 sheet of nori (seaweed)
- Soy sauce (optional)
- Small saucepan with a lid
- Fork
- Cutting board and knife
- Bowl of water (to dip your fingers)

SUSHi RiCe

GROWN-UPS!
Do Step 1.

✱1. Boil the **rice** and **water**. Stir the water when it boils, then reduce the heat to low and cover the **pan**. Let it simmer for 20 minutes.

2. Turn off the heat and leave the covered saucepan alone for 10 more minutes. Then uncover it and let it cool.

3. While the rice is still warm, sprinkle on the **seasoned-rice vinegar** and fluff the rice with a **fork**.

Burrito

GROWN-UPS!
Do Step 1 & 6.

✱1. Slice the **ham**, **mozzarella**, **romaine**, and **pineapple** into strips. Have the other ingredients ready on a work surface.

2. Place the **nori**, with the shiny side down and add ¾ cup (180 mL) of **sushi rice** on the center.

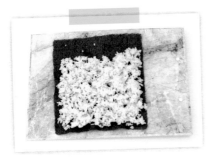

3. Wet your fingers and spread the rice evenly to the edges of the nori, leaving the top fourth uncovered.

4. Lay the fillings in a line centered on the rice. Use your fingers to wet the top of the nori sheet where there is no rice.

5. Use both hands to lift the burrito from the bottom. Fold it over and, with a little pressure, roll it up. When the bottom touches the wet part of the nori, hold it for about 10 seconds so the nori sticks together.

✱6. Slice the burrito in half and serve it with a little **soy sauce** for dipping.

SALAD DRESSING
SCIENCE

Mix and match ingredients to serve up your own custom creation.

Bee's Knees

EMULSIFIERS (ee-**MULL**-suh-fires) are needed whenever you mix oil with something like water or vinegar. Normally, oil and water drops stay separate. Try whisking together just the oil and vinegar— they won't blend until you add an emulsifier.

YOU WILL NEED

MAKES
1 JAR OF
DRESSING

Prep Time:
10 minutes

Acid
(use amount
in the chart)

Emulsifier
(see chart)

Oil
(see chart)

Rainbow
Whisk

Mixing
bowl

1. In a mixing bowl add the **acid** and the **emulsifier** from the chart and mix them well with your **rainbow whisk**. You can add a pinch of salt, if you'd like.

2. Very slowly add the **oil** in a thin stream while constantly mixing with your rainbow whisk to emulsify. Whisk as fast as you can without spilling.

3. Toss the dressing with green salad, or bottle it in a jar and store it in the fridge. Use the sticker in the front of this book to label your salad dressing jar!

WIN-WIN VINAIGRETTE	CITRUS BLISS	BEE'S KNEES DRESSING
¼ cup (60 mL) balsamic vinegar	¼ cup (60 mL) orange juice	¼ cup (60 mL) apple cider vinegar
+ 1 Tbsp (15 mL) Dijon mustard	½ tsp (2.5 mL) red-wine vinegar	+ 1½ Tbsp (22 mL) honey
+ ¾ cup (180 mL) extra-virgin olive oil	+ 1½ Tbsp (22 mL) miso paste	+ ¾ cup (180 mL) unrefined peanut oil*
	+ ¾ cup (180 mL) avocado oil	*If you don't eat peanuts, use a different oil. Do not use peanut oil meant for frying.

ACID =   EMULSIFIER =   OIL =

MOVIE NIGHT
POPCORN

Pop! Pop! Make this for your next movie marathon.

Find this sticker in the front of the book!

POP-CORN

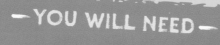

— YOU WILL NEED —

2/3 cup (160 mL) popcorn kernels (or fewer—only pop as many kernels as can fit in a single layer on the bottom of your saucepan)

2 Tbsp (30 mL) vegetable oil

3 Tbsp (45 mL) butter (optional)

Deep saucepan with a tight-fitting lid

Salt (optional)

SERVES: LOTS

Prep Time: 20 minutes

GROWN-UPS! Do Steps 1–3 with your kid chef.

TIP
Olive oil is perfect for this recipe, but feel free to use a different kind of oil.

✳1. Pour the **oil** into the **saucepan** and place it on high heat. Put a **kernel** in the oil, and listen closely. When it pops, the oil is ready.

Hot oil is dangerous. Make sure your pan is dry (water can cause splatters) and keep your distance while the oil heats up.

✳2. Add the rest of the kernels and cover the pan with the lid. Gently shake the pan so all the kernels are covered in oil. You'll hear the kernels start popping!

✳3. When the popping finally slows down, you're ready to turn off the heat and pour the popped popcorn into a bowl. You can sprinkle **salt** and a little **melted butter** over the top, if you'd like.

OPTIONAL: Peanut Butter Topping

Melt 3 Tbsp (45 mL) of butter over low heat, and add 3 Tbsp (45 mL) of chunky peanut butter (or sunflower-seed butter) so it all melts together. Use a big spoon to drizzle it over the **popcorn**.

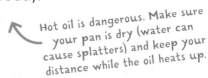

FAMILY DINNER

Little Chicken
DRUMETTES

Mmmm . . .
tastes like chicken!

—YOU WILL NEED—

1/4 cup (60 mL) ketchup

1/4 cup (60 mL) barbecue sauce

Juice of 1 lemon

12 chicken drumettes (they look like tiny drumsticks)

Oven mitts

Mixing bowl

Tongs

Rainbow whisk

Baking sheet and tinfoil

MAKES 4 SERVINGS

Prep Time: 10 minutes

Bake: 30 minutes

TIP
If you can't find drumettes, small chicken wings are fine, too!

GROWN-UPS! Do Step 1.

STEP 1

Preheat the oven to 350°F (175°C). Cover your **baking sheet** with **tinfoil**.

STEP 2

Whisk the **ketchup**, **barbecue sauce**, and **lemon juice** in the mixing bowl.

STEP 3

Add the **chicken drumettes** and stir to coat them evenly with sauce.

STEP 4

GROWN-UPS! Do Step 4.

Spread the coated drumettes on the baking sheet and bake for 30 minutes. Use **oven mitts** when taking the chicken out of the oven, and set the sheet on a heat-proof surface. Use **tongs** to place the chicken on a plate.

TIP
After handling raw chicken, always wash your hands and any tools you touched with warm, soapy water.

OODLES of NOODLES

Share these slightly sweet sesame-flavored noodles with the whole family.

— YOU WILL NEED —

1 lb (450 g) box of spaghetti noodles

1/2 cup (125 mL) creamy peanut butter

1 Tbsp (15 mL) sesame oil

2 Tbsp (30 mL) soy sauce

4 Tbsp (60 mL) water

1 Tbsp (15 mL) honey

Dash of hot sauce (optional)

Toasted sesame seeds

Large pot of water

Colander

Mixing bowl

Rainbow whisk

Tongs

TIP
If you don't eat peanut butter, you can use sunflower-seed butter instead.

GROWN-UPS! Do Step 1.

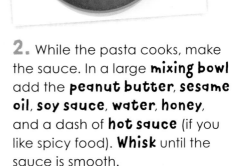

1. Bring a large **pot of water** to a boil, add the **dry spaghetti**, and let it boil for about 10 minutes. (Check the package to see if they recommend more or less time.) Then drain the cooked noodles into a **colander** and rinse with cold **water**.

2. While the pasta cooks, make the sauce. In a large **mixing bowl** add the **peanut butter, sesame oil, soy sauce, water, honey,** and a dash of **hot sauce** (if you like spicy food). **Whisk** until the sauce is smooth.

3. Place the noodles in the bowl of sauce and use **tongs** to coat the noodles really well.

4. Divide the noodles into individual bowls. Top each serving with some **toasted sesame seeds** (and a garnish of fresh cilantro, if you'd like) and enjoy!

Fiesta Fish Tacos

Fish isn't just tasty—it's also fun to make!

Did You Know...
Yummy Hum
When hunting for fish to eat, sharks listen for a low-frequency pulse called the "yummy hum." Humans can't hear it (too bad for us!).

YOU WILL NEED

1 lb (450 g) of codfish or snapper fillets

3/4 cup (100 g) dry bread crumbs

2 eggs

1/4 cup (60 mL) butter or margarine

Tortillas

1 cup (250 mL) chopped lettuce

Toppings such as sour cream, cheese, or guacamole (optional)

wax paper and paper towels

Knife and cutting board

Plate

Bowl

Rainbow whisk

Spatula

Baking pan and oven mitts

Saucepan or microwave-safe bowl

TIP
You can use plain or seasoned bread crumbs—it's up to you!

GROWN-UPS! Do Step 1.

1. Preheat the oven to 400°F (205°C). Wash the **fillets**, then pat them dry with **paper towels**. Cut them up into long pieces, and then into chunks.

2. Spread the **bread crumbs** on a **plate** covered with **wax paper**. Break the **eggs** into a **bowl** and **whisk** them.

GROWN-UPS! Do Steps 4 & 5.

3. Dip each piece of fish into the eggs, then roll it in the bread crumbs until it's coated. Then lay it on the **baking pan**.

4. Melt the **butter** in the microwave on medium power in bursts of 20–30 seconds, or on the stove. Pour a little butter over each piece of fish.

5. Bake the fish until golden brown, about 15 minutes. Use oven mitts and set the pan on a heat-proof surface.

6. Assemble each taco as follows: **tortilla**, a few pieces of fish, and any extra toppings.

FRI-YAY
Fries

Serve up these colorful veggie fries any day of the week!

— YOU WILL NEED —

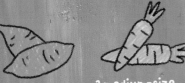

2 sweet potatoes

2 medium-size carrots

2 Tbsp (30 mL) vegetable oil

Salt and pepper to taste

Vegetable peeler

Cutting board

Knife

Tongs

Baking pan, tinfoil, and oven mitts

Mixing bowl

MAKES 4–6 SERVINGS

Prep & Bake Time: 1 hour

TIP
Olive oil works great in this recipe, but you can use another type of vegetable oil, if you'd like.

✳1. Wash and dry all the **veggies**. Preheat your oven to 400°F (205°C).

GROWN-UPS!
Do Step 1 & 2.

✳2. Peel the veggies. Cut each **carrot** into 4 pieces, and each **potato** into about 8 wedges.

3. Put all the pieces into a **mixing bowl**, then add the **oil** and a little bit of **salt** and **pepper**. Gently mix them together to coat the veggies. You may need to use your hands.

GROWN-UPS!
Do Step 4.

✳4. Place the veggies on a **foil-coated pan** in one thin layer. Bake them for 45 minutes total, until they're brown and crispy. After 20 minutes, use **tongs** to flip them over. Remember **oven mitts** when taking out the pan! Let them cool a little before serving.

ZUCCHINI VARIATION

If you have room on your pan for more fries, add this variation: slice one zucchini in half, and then into wedges. Whisk an egg in a bowl, then coat each fry in egg batter and bread crumbs, just like the fish on page 51.

CURRY in a HURRY

This not-too-spicy stew has a lot of flavors. Taste test it as you go!

GARAM MASALA

In the Hindi language "garam masala" means "warm spice mix." Garam masala is a mix of different spices, including bay leaf, cardamom, cinnamon, cloves, cumin, and peppercorns. It comes from India and Pakistan, and you can usually find it in your local grocery store.

YOU WILL NEED

MAKES 6 SERVINGS

Prep Time: 30 minutes

Bake: 20 minutes

 6 hotdogs

 14.5 oz (406 g) can whole plum tomatoes

 1 large leaf of green kale

 1-inch (2.5 cm) piece of ginger

 3 cloves of garlic

 1 small red onion

 2 Tbsp (30 mL) vegetable oil

 1 tsp (5 mL) garam masala spice

 15 oz (420 g) can of garbanzo beans

 1 Tbsp (15 mL) salt

 1/2 cup (125 mL) water

 Cutting board and knife

 Medium casserole dish

 Bowl

 Spoon

Tongs

GROWN-UPS! Do Step 1.

✴1. Cut each **hot dog** in half. To create arms, cut ¾ of the way into the hot dog. Then roll the hot dog and make two more cuts side by side.

2. Tear the whole **tomatoes** in a **bowl**. Tear off the leafy part of the **kale** from the stem. Scrape the **ginger** peel off with a **spoon**.

GROWN-UPS! Do Step 3-6.

✴3. Chop the **garlic** and **ginger** into tiny pieces. Cut the **red onion** in half, top to bottom, and then into slices.

✴4. Place the pot over high heat, add **oil**, and wait 1 minute. Reduce the heat to medium, and add the hot dogs. Cook them in the hot oil, turning every 20 seconds for 3 minutes. The ends will curl up. Turn off the heat and use **tongs** to remove the octo-dogs to a plate lined with a paper towel.

✴5. Add **ginger**, **onion**, **garlic**, and **garam masala** to the remaining oil in the pan and turn the heat up to medium. Cook for about 1 minute, until the edges start to look golden.

7. Serve the curry in bowls, and add two "octo-dogs" to each bowl.

✴6. Once the **onion** is soft, add the tomato, **chickpeas**, and **water**. Stir, add the **kale**, and simmer. Add a pinch of **salt** and a pinch of garam masala. Cover the pot and cook for 5 minutes.

RAINBOW PIZZA

Swap the veggies on this pizza with any other toppings you'd like!

Easy-Peasy Pizzas
You can use English muffins instead of dough, if you prefer. Slice a muffin in half, then top each side with sauce and veggies. Bake your topped English muffins at 400°F (205°C) for 15-20 minutes (just until the cheese melts).

— YOU WILL NEED —

MAKES
4–6
SERVINGS

Prep Time:
30 minutes
Bake:
30 minutes

2 Tbsp (30 mL) vegetable oil

Pizza dough (store-bought or from scratch on page 58)

8 oz can (224 mL) of tomato sauce

1/2 tsp (2.5 mL) dried basil

1/2 tsp (2.5 mL) oregano

1/4 pound (112 g) shredded mozzarella cheese

1/4 cup (60 mL) each of sliced cherry tomatoes, orange pepper, corn kernels, broccoli, and chopped red onion

Baking sheet

Rolling pin (optional)

Mixing bowl

Rainbow whisk

Big spoon

Oven mitts

1. Preheat your oven to 425°F (218°C). Rub a little **oil** on a **baking sheet**. Divide your **dough** into 4 pieces for small pizzas now, or make 1 big pizza.

2. Roll or stretch the dough to cover the **pan**. Go slow to make a nice even crust. The edges should be a little thicker.

3. In a mixing bowl, **whisk** together the **tomato sauce** with the **dried basil** and **oregano** to make pizza sauce.

4. Use a big **spoon** to spread the sauce around the pizza. Then top the pizza with the **cheese** and your **veggies** in rainbow order.

GROWN-UPS! Do Step 5.

✳**5.** Bake your pizza for 30 minutes; the crust will just slightly darken. Take out the pan while you're wearing **oven mitts**, set on a heat-proof surface, and let your pizza cool for a bit before cutting.

DOUGH
from scratch

Level up your pizza skills by making your own dough.

MAKES
4–6
SERVINGS

Prep Time:
15 minutes
Bake:
1 hour

— YOU WILL NEED —

1/4 oz (7 g)
packet dry yeast

1 tsp (5 mL) sugar

3/4 cup (180 mL)
warm water

2 1/2 cups (350 g) flour
plus a little extra

1/2 tsp (2.5 mL) salt

2 Tbsp (30 mL)
vegetable oil

Mixing bowl

Mixing spoon

Clean kitchen towel

1. Put the **yeast** and **sugar** in the **mixing bowl** with the **warm water** and let them sit for 5 minutes until the mixture looks foamy.

2. Add the **flour**, **salt**, and **oil** to the bowl. Mix everything together.

4. Place the dough in a clean bowl, cover it with a **towel**, and let it rise in a warm, dry place about 1 hour until it doubles in size.

3. Place the **dough** onto a lightly floured surface. Turn the dough over and over, pressing the palm of your hand into the center of the dough, then folding the sides into the middle. This is called kneading. Do this about 100 times. You can do it!

5. Ta-da! You just made pizza dough. Go ahead and follow the instructions on page 57 to finish making your pizza.

MAKE PRETZELS!
Take your dough at Step 5 and roll it into snakes. Twist them however you'd like. Then whisk one egg in a bowl; with a kitchen brush, brush the egg wash onto your pretzels, and bake in a 400°F (205°C) oven for about 20-25 minutes.

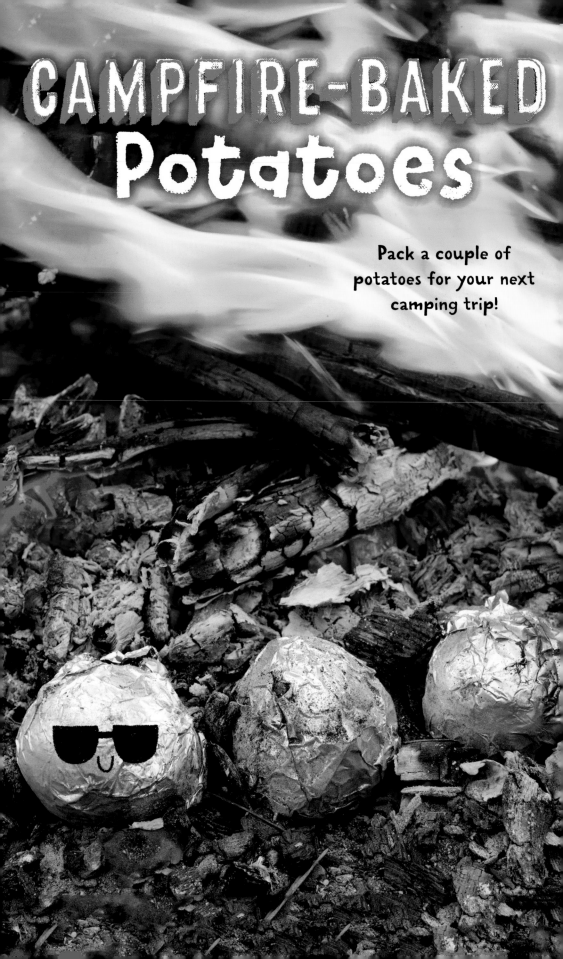

CAMPFIRE-BAKED Potatoes

Pack a couple of potatoes for your next camping trip!

MAKES 4 SERVINGS

Prep Time: 10 minutes
Bake: 45–90 minutes

4 baking potatoes

Butter

Fork

Tinfoil

Long stick or shovel

Oven mitts

GROWN-UPS! Do Step 1.

1. Prepare your fire. When the ashes or coals start to turn white, it's the perfect temperature to cook your potatoes. You'll bake them in the ashes, not in the fire.

Grown-ups should use proper precaution building and extinguishing the campfire. Use only established areas of camping grounds.

2. Use the **fork** tines to poke a few holes all around the **potatoes**.

GROWN-UPS! Do Step 4.

3. Cut a piece of **tinfoil** big enough to wrap each potato in. Smear some **butter** all around each potato's skin.

4. Wrap the foil tightly around each potato. Use a long stick or shovel to dig a little hole in the campfire ashes. Bury the potatoes and let them bake in the ashes until they're a little soft when you poke them with a stick. It usually takes 45 minutes. Use your stick or shovel and **oven mitts** to remove the hot potato.

Potatoes at Home

If you don't have a campfire handy, this recipe works great in an oven, too. Grown-ups, preheat your oven to 400°F (205°C). Follow Steps 2–4, but place the potatoes on the oven rack (no pan) to bake for 45–60 minutes. Use oven mitts to check and remove the potatoes. When the potato is squeezable, it's done!

DESSERTS

TIP

Wrap cookies in a cellophane bag and seal with a cute sticker from this book.

CHOCOLATE CHIP
COOKIES

FROZEN
BANANOIDS

Chocolate and bananas go together like BFFs!

— YOU WILL NEED —

4–5 bananas

Toppings of your choice:
1 cup (250 mL) chopped walnuts,
shredded coconut, or sprinkles

1 cup (250 mL) chocolate chips

Cutting board and knife

Prep Time: 30 minutes
Bake: 30 minutes

12–15 Popsicle sticks

2+ bowls for toppings

2 large plates

Wax paper

Double boiler or microwave-safe bowl

Rainbow whisk

GROWN-UPS! Do Steps 1, 2 & 3.

1. Peel each **banana**, cut it in three pieces, and push a **Popsicle stick** through the center of each banana piece. You now have bananoids.

2. Put each of your toppings in a separate **bowl**. **GROWN-UPS** should chop the **walnuts** if you use them. Cover a **large plate** with **wax paper.**

3. Slowly melt the **chocolate chips**, either on the stove top with a **double boiler**, or in the microwave with a microwave-safe bowl.

MICROWAVE: Pour chocolate chips into your bowl. Microwave it in bursts of 30 seconds at a time, and stir really, really well with your whisk in between microwaving.

DOUBLE BOILER: Put 1–1 ½ cups of water into the bottom pan, and pour the chocolate into the top pan. Turn the heat on low, and stir a lot for about 5 minutes, or until the chocolate is all melted.

4. Now the gooey part. Holding a bananoid by the Popsicle stick, dip it into the chocolate. Then roll it around in the toppings of your choice, and set it on the wax paper-covered plate. This recipe fills about two plates.

5. Put the filled plates in the freezer and wait as long as you can stand it.

RRRAW-SOME COOKIE DOUGH

No flour, no eggs, no problem.

TIP
Refrigerate any leftovers.

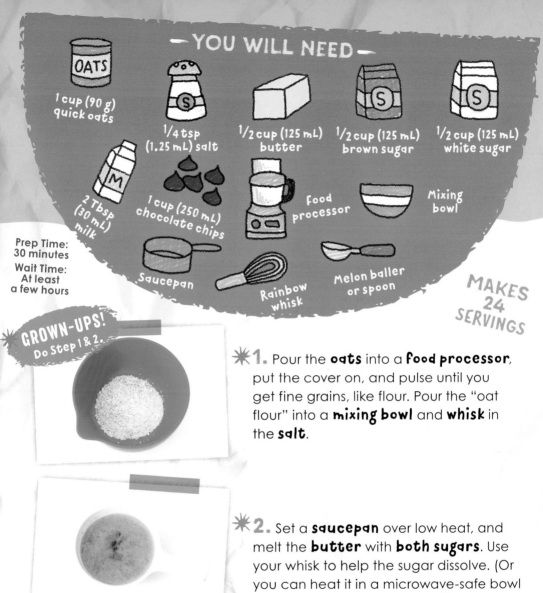

— YOU WILL NEED —

OATS
1 cup (90 g) quick oats

1/4 tsp (1.25 mL) salt

1/2 cup (125 mL) butter

1/2 cup (125 mL) brown sugar

1/2 cup (125 mL) white sugar

2 Tbsp (30 mL) milk

1 cup (250 mL) chocolate chips

Food processor

Mixing bowl

Saucepan

Rainbow whisk

Melon baller or spoon

Prep Time:
30 minutes

Wait Time:
At least a few hours

MAKES 24 SERVINGS

GROWN-UPS! Do Step 1 & 2.

1. Pour the **oats** into a **food processor**, put the cover on, and pulse until you get fine grains, like flour. Pour the "oat flour" into a **mixing bowl** and **whisk** in the **salt**.

2. Set a **saucepan** over low heat, and melt the **butter** with **both sugars**. Use your whisk to help the sugar dissolve. (Or you can heat it in a microwave-safe bowl for 30-second bursts at a low setting.)

3. Take the saucepan off the heat, then stir in the **milk**. Stir the butter mixture into the finely ground oatmeal. Cover the bowl and let it sit in the fridge so the oats absorb the liquid. (Waiting overnight will make a softer dough, but it's OK to taste test before it's done.)

4. Let your dough sit out until it's just soft enough to fold in the **chocolate chips**. Use a **melon baller** or **spoon** to help shape the dough into bite-size pieces.

CHOCOLATE chomp! COOKIES

This recipe deserves your immediate attention.

- YOU WILL NEED -

MAKES 24 SERVINGS

Prep Time: 30 minutes
Bake: 12 minutes
Wait Time: 1 hour

 1/2 cup (125 mL) butter

 1/2 cup (125 mL) brown sugar

 1/2 cup (125 mL) white sugar

 1 cup + 2 Tbsp (160 g) flour

 1/2 tsp (2.5 mL) baking soda

 1/4 tsp (1.25 mL) salt

1 egg

 1 tsp (5 mL) vanilla extract

 1 cup (250 mL) chocolate chips

 Small saucepan

 Rainbow whisk

 Mixing bowl

 Small bowl

Cookie sheet

 Oven mitts

 Spatula

GROWN-UPS!
Do Steps 1 & 6.

*1. In a small **saucepan**, melt the **butter**. While it's warm, add **both sugars**. Stir, then let it cool a bit.

2. Mix the **flour, baking soda,** and **salt** in the **mixing bowl**.

3. In the small bowl, **whisk** the **egg** lightly, then add the egg and **vanilla** to the butter mixture.

4. Add the wet ingredients to the dry mixture. Stir again, then add **chocolate chips**.

5. Stir everything well and put the bowl in the refrigerator to cool for an hour. About 5–10 minutes before you take it out, turn your oven on to 375°F (190°C).

TIP
You can mix a few candies or sprinkles into your dough, too! Use Kick-the-Can Ice Cream (page 74) to make ice cream sandwiches.

*6. Roll the dough into walnut-size balls, put them on the ungreased **cookie sheet**, and bake for 10 minutes. Wear **oven mitts** when handling the hot pan. Remove the cookies with the **spatula**, and let them cool.

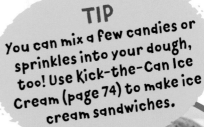

Best-Ever brownies

Treat yourself! Fudgy brownies are also perfect for sharing with others.

YOU WILL NEED

1 cup (250 mL) butter + extra to grease the pan

¾ cup (64 g) cocoa powder

2 cups (400 g) sugar

4 eggs

1 tsp (5 mL) vanilla extract

1 ¼ cups (175 g) all-purpose flour

¼ tsp (1.25 mL) salt

Confectioner's sugar (optional)

8- or 9-inch square baking pan

Rainbow whisk

Small saucepan

Mixing bowl

Oven mitts

Prep Time: 20 minutes

Bake: 40–50 minutes

GROWN-UPS!
Do Step 2 & 6.

1. Preheat your oven to 350°F (175°C). Unwrap the **butter** and use the buttery side of the paper to grease the **pan**.

✸**2.** Meanwhile, melt the butter over a low heat in a small **saucepan**. Watch it. It's easy to burn.

3. In your **mixing bowl**, **whisk** the **cocoa** and **sugar** together. Then stir in the melted butter. Add the **eggs** and **vanilla**, and stir again.

4. Now add the **flour** and **salt**, and mix just until smooth. Don't mix too much.

5. Scrape the mixture into the pan and spread it out in an even layer. Bake for 40–50 minutes, or until the brownies just begin to pull away from the sides of the pan.

✸**6.** Take the pan out of the oven with **oven mitts**, then let it cool on a heat-proof surface before cutting. Sprinkle a little **confectioner's sugar** to decorate.

Rock Candy LAB

A science experiment you can eat! Rock candy takes a few weeks to grow, so you'll need to plan ahead.

YOU WILL NEED:

Prep Time: 15 minutes

Wait Time: 2–3 weeks

½ cup (125 mL) water

1 cup (120 g) sugar

Food coloring (optional)

Tall glass jar

Cotton string

Chopstick or Popsicle stick

Rainbow whisk

Scissors

Small saucepan

GROWN-UPS!
Do Steps 1–3.

✴**1.** Put the **water** into the **saucepan** and bring it to a boil on the stove.

✴**2.** Turn off the heat and immediately add **sugar** to the saucepan. **Whisk** for 2 minutes until the sugar is dissolved. The liquid should be clear, but if you'd like, you can add a drop of **food coloring** now.

✴**3.** Carefully pour the mixture into the tall **jar**. Cut a piece of **string** 2 or 3 times the height of your jar. Tie one end of the string to the **chopstick**. Then lay the chopstick across the mouth of the jar, with the string inside. The dangling end can coil around the bottom of the jar.

4. Leave the jar on the counter for 2–3 weeks to let the candy crystals grow. You can lift the string out of the jar every few days to check on it, but make sure to put it back in the sugar mixture. When you're happy with the amount of crystals that have grown on your string, remove it, and hang it up to dry.

Troubleshooting
The scientists at Klutz Labs have a few tricks for making rock candy. Braiding the string in Step 3 can help because it gives the crystals more area to grow on. You can also dip the string into water and roll it in loose sugar to "seed" the crystals before you dip it into cooled sugar water.

Kick-the-can Ice Cream

Beat the heat with this summery treat!

YOU WILL NEED

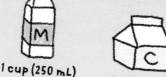

 1 cup (250 mL) whole milk

 1 cup (250 mL) heavy cream

 ½ cup (125 mL) sugar

 4+ cups (1+ L) ice cubes

 Duct-tape

4 lb (1.8 kg) box of ice cream salt (also called rock salt)

1 small coffee can

 1 big coffee can

MAKES 4–6 Servings

Prep Time: 30 minutes (more if you freeze it)

1. Pour the **milk, heavy cream,** and **sugar** into the **small coffee can**. Put the lid on, and **duct-tape** it closed. You don't want your ice cream to spill when it rolls!

2. Pour a little bit of **rock salt** and a few **ice cubes** into the bottom of your **large coffee can**. Nest the small coffee can inside, and fill up the sides with the rest of the ice cubes and salt.

3. Put the lid on the large coffee can, and tape down the lid really, really securely. Then roll the can across the ground for about 20 minutes. It's good to do this with a friend, preferably outside.

4. Take out the small coffee can and check out the whipped, frosty goodness! You can store the can in the freezer and let the ice cream firm up a bit before you serve it.

If you don't have coffee cans, you can use a quart-size ziplock bag inside a gallon-size ziplock bag. Make sure to seal the bags really, really well.

How does it work?

Mixing salt with ice cubes is amazingly colder than just ice alone. (It's the same reason why you see people spread salt on icy roads—the ice lowers the melting temperature of the water.) The salt-slush mixture is colder than regular freezing and super-chills your ice cream ingredients while they churn, or mix together.

HOW TO
Set a Table

Wow your family and guests with a fancy-schmancy table setting.

PLACE CARD with the sitter's name

DRINK on the right, above the big plate

SALAD BOWL or BREAD PLATE on the left, above the big plate

KRISTIN

BIG PLATE or BOWL in the middle

FOLDED NAPKIN and FORK on the left

KNIFE and SPOON on the right

MAKE YOUR OWN
Place Cards

Trace this template and cut out a little rectangle of paper. Fold it in half, then decorate one side with your guest's name. Make one place card for each person at the table.

MENU

Jot down ideas about what you want to make!

Monday

Tuesday

Wednesday

Thursday

Friday

Saturday

Sunday

CREDITS

Editor: Caitlin Harpin

Designer and Illustrator: Lizzy Doyle

Photographer: Lucy Schaeffer

Additional Tech Photos:
The editors of Klutz

Package Designer: Owen Keating

Buyers: Kelly Shaffer and Vicky Eva

Models: Erin H., Mabel M., Shane M., Talia P., and Tyler R.

Recipe Inspiration: Linda Bliss, Laurie Cardella, Nancy Cassidy, Paul Doherty, Gerilyn Ewing, Prakesh Garties, Sarah Gilman, Sandy Goosen, Jeanne Heise, Anne Akers Johnson, Connie Kuge, Jean Lebbert, Betty Lowman, Jennifer Presley, Kim Raftery, Eleanor Sviatopolk-Mirsky

Food Stylist and Additional Recipe Development: Christopher Barsch

Prop Stylists: Martha Bernabe and Beth Pakradooni

Additional Food Prep: Rachel McPherson-McLaughlin

Testers: Brianna Austin, Armin Bautista, Brian Cardella, Jason Cardella, Sarah Cardella, Courtney deVerges, Emily Feliberty, J. Tim Gallagher, Rachel Gold, Owen Keating, Benjamin Krislov, Eva L., Annie McAndrew, Molly McAndrew, Derrick Miller-Handley, Melisa Miller-Handley, Michael Miller-Handley, Avery S., Kim Ryon, Mimi Oey, Linda Olbourne, Elizabeth Rein-Podgorski, Julia Romero, and Megan Seccombe

Product Development:
April Chorba, Netta Rabin, Hannah Rogge, and Stacy Lellos

Get creative with more from KLUTZ

Looking for more goof-proof activities, sneak peeks, and giveaways? Find us online!

Klutz Books   Klutz Books   Klutz   @KlutzBooks   @KlutzBooks

Klutz.com • thefolks@klutz.com • 1-800-737-4123